German Cookbook

25 Delicious German Food Recipes to Please your Taste Buds

Try the Best German Recipes

By

Martha Stone

Copyright 2016 Martha Stone

License Notes

No part of this Book can be reproduced in any form or by any means including print, electronic, scanning or photocopying unless prior permission is granted by the author.

All ideas, suggestions and guidelines mentioned here are written for informative purposes. While the author has taken every possible step to ensure accuracy, all readers are advised to follow information at their own risk. The author cannot be held responsible for personal and/or commercial damages in case of misinterpreting and misunderstanding any part of this Book.

About the author

Martha Stone is a chef and also cookbook writer. She was born and raised in Idaho where she spent most of her life growing up. Growing up in the country taught her how to appreciate and also use fresh ingredients in her cooking. This love for using the freshest ingredients turned into a passion for cooking. Martha loves to teach others how to cook and she loves every aspect of cooking from preparing the dish to smelling it cooking and sharing it with friends.

Martha eventually moved to California and met the love of her life. She settled down and has two children. She is a stay at home mom and involves her children in her cooking as much as possible. Martha decided to start writing cookbooks so that she could share her love for food and cooking with everyone else.

For a complete list of my published books, please, visit my Author's Page...

http://amzn.to/1QAkZpV

Table of Contents

Introduction 7
Chapter 01: Soups and Stews 8
    Apple Cider Soup with Little Cheese Puffs 9
    Berlin Potato Soup 12
    Beef Goulash Soup 15
    Autumn Vegetable Beef Stew 17
    Bavarian Meatball Stew 19
Chapter 02: Meat and Poultry Special 21
    Traditional German Senfbraten 22
    German Schnitzel (Jäger-Schnitzel) 24
    German Beef Rouladen 26
    Chicken Schnitzel with Creamy Potato Salad 28
    German Peasant Style Chicken 30
Chapter 03: Seafood and Fish Recipes 32
    Seared Salmon & Green Potato Salad 33
    German Fish with Sauerkraut 35
    German Beer Fish (Bier Fisch) 37
    Bavarian Smelts 39
    Eel in Dill Sauce 41
Chapter 04: Sauces and Salads 43
    Jägerschnitzel Sauce 44
    German Zigeunerschnitzel 46
    German Green Sauce (Grune Sosse) 48

Sauerkraut Salad 50
  Warm German Potato Salad 52
Chapter 05: Delicious Desserts 54
  German Baby 55
  German Apple Cake 57
  Old German Honey Cookies 59
  German Marble Cake 61
  German Iced Coffee 63
Conclusion 64
Author's Afterthoughts 65

Introduction

This book is simply a German cookbook. I've spent a considerable time of my life in Germany and during my time there, I tried all kinds of German food recipes. I fell in love with almost everything that I ate there. I have shared in this book some of the best German recipes and the ones that I really love. I hope you too, like me, will fall in love with German cuisine.

Chapter 01: Soups and Stews

Apple Cider Soup with Little Cheese Puffs

Cooking time: At least an hour

Serving size: Four servings

Description: This soup is rich with creamy and fruity flavor. The flavor is balanced by the addition of these yummy airy cheese puffs which make the soup beautiful.

Ingredients:

For the cheese puffs:

- Butter (2 tbsp.)
- 2 eggs
- Grated Allgäuer Emmentaler (3.5 oz.) (You can use some other German cheese too)
- Flour (2/3 cup)
- Water (1/2 cup)

For the soup:

- Unsalted butter (3 tbsp.)
- Sugar (1 pinch)
- Heavy cream (1 liter)
- Apple cider (1 liter)
- Flour (1/4 cup)
- Freshly ground pepper

Directions:

For the cheese puffs:

1. Preheat your oven to 350°F.

2. Take a medium saucepan and boil butter and salt in water.

3. Add the flour to the saucepan. Stir the mixture until it becomes compact and solid as a lump.

4. Now, remove the dough from heat, add the grated cheese and let it cool down to room temperature.

5. Now add eggs and stir the mixture until it is smooth.

6. Place a piece of parchment on the cookie tray and make small mounds on it using a pastry bag with a star-shaped tip.

7. Bake for about 7 to 8 minutes or until they are golden brown.

For the soup:

1. Melt butter in a saucepan.

2. Add flour in the butter and stir it until it's smooth.

3. Slowly add apple cider and let the mixture simmer for 5 minutes.

4. Add lemon juice, cream, a pinch of pepper and sugar to the mixture. Stir.

5. Pour the soup into soup bowls and place the puffs on top.

6. The puffs would float on the surface. Enjoy!!

Berlin Potato Soup

Cooking time: 1 hour and 15 minutes

Serving size: 5 servings

Description: You can think of this delicious soup as the German version of the vegetable soup. It's really delicious and nutritious because of all the vegetables it has.

Ingredients:

- Mealy potatoes (1.3 lb.)
- Carrots (7.1 oz.)
- Streaky bacon (3.5 oz.)
- Vegetable stock (4 cups)
- Oil (4 tsp)
- 1 leek
- 1/2 celery root (You can use celery ribs too)
- 1 big onion
- 1 parsley root
- 1 bailey leaf
- 4 wiener sausages
- Caraway (1/3 tsp)
- Marjoram (1/3 tsp)
- freshly ground pepper
- Nutmeg

Directions:

1. Wash all the veggies.

2. Start with peeling and chopping the onion.

3. Peel the potatoes and then dice them.

4. Slice the leek.

5. Peel the carrots and chop them.

6. Chop the parsley roots and celery.

7. Dice the bacon. Heat the oil in a deep pan and put the diced bacon in it.

8. Add chopped onion and sauté until the onion is translucent.

9. Now, add the vegetables and cook them for 10 minutes.

10. Add vegetable stock, caraway and marjoram. Cook this for 30 minutes.

11. Add the vegetables and garnish with freshly ground black pepper.

12. Add the sliced sausages to the soup and let them cook in the soup.

13. Pour into bowls. Garnish with freshly chopped parsley.

14. Serve with roasted onions. If you like, you can serve with fresh coarse rye bread too.

Beef Goulash Soup

Cooking time: 1 hour and 10 minutes

Serving size: 16 servings

Description: For the beef lovers, this recipe is just too good. You would forget your beef soups after having this one!

Ingredients:

- Beef top sirloin steak, (2 pounds) (Cut the beef into cubes, half an inch each)
- 1 big chopped green pepper
- 1 big chopped onion
- 3 medium chopped carrots
- 3 medium potatoes (Peel them and cut them into cubes)
- Olive oil (2 tbsp.)
- Beef broth (4 cups)
- Water (1 cup)
- Sugar (1 tbsp.)
- Salt (1-2 tsp or to taste)
- Black pepper (1/2 tsp)
- Paprika (2 tbsp.)
- Cayenne pepper (1/2 tsp)
- 2 bay leaves
- 1 can tomato paste (6 oz.)
- 1 can crushed tomatoes (28 oz.)

- Caraway seeds (2 tbsp.)
- Sour cream

Directions:

1. Heat oil in a Dutch oven and cook beef, green pepper and onion in it over medium-high heat.

2. When the meat is all brown, drain.

3. Now add carrots, potatoes, olive oil, beef broth, water, sugar, salt, black pepper, paprika and cayenne pepper. Bring them to boil.

4. Lower the heat and cover it. Let the soup simmer for 25 to 30 minutes. Make sure the potatoes are tender.

5. Add the bay leaves, tomato paste and crushed tomatoes in the soup and stir them in.

6. Cover the soup again and let it simmer for another 25 to 30 minutes until the meat is soft and tender.

7. Remove the bay leaves and discard them.

8. When serving, top each bowl of this incredible soup with sour cream!

9. Enjoy!

Autumn Vegetable Beef Stew

Cooking time: 2 hours

Serving size: 4 servings

Description: This is an excellent German recipe. You can enjoy it with homemade bread and salad.

Ingredients:

- Round steak (1 pound) (Cut it into cubes, one-inch each)
- Canola oil (1 tbsp.)
- All-purpose flour (1 tbsp.)
- Water (1-1/2 cups)
- Paprika (1/4 tsp)
- Salt (1 tsp)
- Pepper (1/4 tsp)
- 1 bay leaf
- 2 beef bouillon cubes
- 1 medium chopped onion
- Caraway seeds (1/2 tsp)
- Tomato sauce (1/2 cup)
- 2 medium peeled potatoes (Cut them into cubes, one-inch each)
- 2 medium peeled carrots (Cut them into slices, one-inch each)
- 2 medium peeled turnips (Cut them into cubes, one-inch each)

Directions:

1. Put the beef in a bowl and toss with paprika, salt and pepper.

2. Now, take a large saucepan and heat the oil in it.

3. Cook beef in the oil over medium heat until it turns brown.

4. Now throw the flour on the beef and stir it well.

5. Add water, tomato sauce, caraway seeds, bouillon, bay leaf and onion in it.

6. Cover the saucepan and let the beef simmer for an hour.

7. Now, add the potatoes, carrots and turnips in the beef.

8. Cook until the beef and the vegetables are tender. This should take 45 minutes.

9. Discard the bay leaf and serve hot.

10. Enjoy!

Bavarian Meatball Stew

Cooking time: 1 hour and 10 minutes

Serving size: 8 servings

Description: This stew is for meatball lovers. You can enjoy it anytime but on a chilly evening, it tastes very homey.

Ingredients:

- 1 lightly beaten egg
- Ground nutmeg (1/4 tsp)
- Black pepper (1/4 tsp)
- Ground allspice (1/4 tsp)
- Dried parsley flakes (3 tbsp.)
- Soft breadcrumbs (1/2 cup)
- 2 cans beef broth (14-1/2 oz. each)
- Ground beef (1-1/2 pounds)
- Pepper (1/2 tsp)
- Sugar (1 tbsp.)
- 1 can Bavarian sauerkraut, (14 oz.) (washed and drained)
- 1 can diced tomatoes (14-1/2 oz.) (undrained)
- 2 medium peeled potatoes (cut them into cubes)
- 2 celery sliced ribs
- 2 medium sliced carrots
- 1 envelope onion soup mix
- 1 bay leaf

Directions:

1. Combine the beaten egg, ground nutmeg, black pepper, ground allspice, parsley and soft breadcrumbs in a large bowl.

2. Add beef and mix the ingredients well.

3. Now make one-inch balls with the mixture.

4. Grease a baking pan and bake the meatballs for 14 minutes at 400°F.

5. In the meantime, combine the remaining ingredients in a saucepan.

6. Add the meatballs when they are baked. Boil.

7. Lower heat and let the stew simmer for 30 to 35 minutes.

8. Discard the bay leaf.

9. Serve and enjoy!

Chapter 02: Meat and Poultry Special

Traditional German Senfbraten

Cooking time: 2 hours and 5 minutes

Serving size: 6 servings

Description:

Ingredients:

- Oil
- Pork roast (2 lb.)
- Beef broth (2 cups)
- German mustard
- 1 large chopped yellow onion
- Butter (2 tbsp.)
- 2 minced garlic cloves
- Dry white wine (¼ cup)
- 1 bay leaf
- 2 carrots (Cut them in half)
- Fresh chopped thyme (1 tsp)

For flour slurry:

- Whisk 3 tablespoons of flour in half cup of beef broth

Directions:

1. Rub the roast with salt and pepper.

2. Then rub the roast with a lot of German mustard.

3. Over a high flame, heat the oil in a Dutch oven.

4. Brown both sides of the roast generously.

5. Now, add butter and onions in it. Cook.

6. Add white wine and boil until it evaporates.

7. Add beef broth, thyme, bay leaf and carrots. Boil.

8. Lower heat and let it simmer for an hour and 30 minutes.

9. Remove the carrots and the bay leaf.

10. Transfer the roast to a platter.

11. Cover with foil to keep it warm.

12. Now, simmer the flour slurry until it becomes thick. Add salt and pepper.

13. Serve the roast with potatoes, gravy and German sauerkraut.

German Schnitzel (Jäger-Schnitzel)

Cooking time: 30 minutes

Serving size: 4 servings

Description: This is a simple and quick recipe that you can try when you want to make dinner quickly.

Ingredients:

- 4 veal cutlets, (Pound them lightly with a meat hammer)
- Lemon juice (1 tbsp.)
- Salt (1/2 tsp)
- Water (3 tbsp.)
- 1 egg
- Breadcrumbs (1 cup)
- Flour (1/2 cup)
- Peanut or vegetable oil (3 tbsp.)
- Butter (3 tbsp.)
- 1 sliced lemon

Directions:

1. Cut off the fat from the meat and clip the edges so that the edges don't curve while cooking.

2. Sprinkle lemon juice and salt on the cutlets.

3. Heat oil and butter in a skillet.

4. Coat each cutlet with flour, dip in egg and roll in the breadcrumbs.

5. Fry each side of the cutlet for 3 minutes.

6. Serve with lemon slices.

German Beef Rouladen

Cooking time: 55 minutes

Serving size: 8 servings

Description: I am a huge beef lover. If you are too, you would find this German recipe very delicious.

Ingredients:

- 8 pieces round steak (4 ounces each) (Pound with a meat hammer to 1/4 inch thickness)
- Salt (2 tsp)
- Freshly ground black pepper (2 tsp)
- Paprika (2 tsp)
- Dijon mustard (1/4 cup)
- Minced onion (1/2 cup)
- Canola oil (3 tbsp.)
- 8 slices of bacon
- Water (1 1/4 cups)
- 1 can beef broth (12 ounce)
- Warm water (1 cup)
- Cornstarch (2 tbsp.)
- Sour cream (1/4 cup)

Directions:

1. Coat one side of each piece of meat with ½ tablespoon of mustard.

2. Season with paprika, pepper, salt and onion.

3. Place one slice of bacon on each piece of meat.

4. Jelly-roll the steaks and pin with toothpicks.

5. In a skillet, heat the canola oil over medium heat.

6. Cook both sides of the pieces of meat until they are brown.

7. Pour in beef broth and water. Boil.

8. Lower heat and let it simmer for 30 minutes.

9. Remove the rolls and collect the liquid in a skillet.

10. Whisk 1 cup of water and corn-starch.

11. Add into the skillet. Keep stirring until it thickens.

12. Add sour cream. Stir.

13. Put the rolls in the sauce. Serve!

Chicken Schnitzel with Creamy Potato Salad

Cooking time: 25 minutes

Serving size: 4 servings

Description: Chicken Schnitzel is one of the favorite dishes among Germans and you will find out why.

Ingredients:

- 4 Chicken Breasts (Boneless and Skinless)
- 2 Farm Eggs (Smoothly beaten)
- Panko Breadcrumbs (1⅓ Cups)
- All-Purpose Flour (3 tbsp.)
- Oil
- Finely chopped parsley (1 large bunch)
- Water
- Salt
- Diced red Potatoes (¾ Pound)
- Mayonnaise (¼ Cup)
- Sweet Pickle Relish (¼ Cup)
- 1 Lemon

Directions:

1. Boil water and salt over high heat. Dice potatoes and boil them.

2. Remove the potatoes from heat when they are tender.

3. Place breadcrumbs and flour in two separate bowls. Season each with salt and pepper.

4. Apply salt and pepper to both sides of the chicken breast.

5. Coat each chicken breast first with flour, then with the beaten egg and finally cover it with breadcrumbs.

6. Heat oil in a pan and cook the chicken breast over medium-high heat. Cook each side for 4 to 6 minutes until they are golden brown.

7. Transfer to a platter. Season with salt and pepper immediately.

8. While you cook the chicken, add mayonnaise, half parsley and sweet pickle relish to the cooked potatoes. Stir to combine.

9. Sprinkle salt and pepper.

10. Serve the chicken with potato salad and lemon slices.

11. Garnish with parsley. Serve.

German Peasant Style Chicken

Cooking time: 1 hour 20 minutes

Serving size: 2 to 4 servings

Description: This is a really easy and extra delicious German recipe for chicken lovers.

Ingredients:

- Chicken pieces (3 lbs.)
- Flour (2 tbsp.)
- 2 eggs
- Sliced mushrooms (1 cup)
- Breadcrumbs (1/2 cup)
- Grated parmesan cheese (1/4 cup)
- Butter (6 tbsp.)
- Milk (1 cup)
- Dry white wine (1/4 cup)
- Salt (2 tsp)
- Pepper (1/2 tsp)

Directions:

1. Add 1 ½ teaspoon of salt and ¼ teaspoon of pepper in an egg. Beat until smooth.

2. Dip the chicken in the egg mixture. Then cover with breadcrumbs mixed with Parmesan.

3. Sauté the chicken in a skillet in 4 tbsp. of butter.

4. Remove when the chicken is brown.

5. Bake the chicken at 350F in an oven.

6. Meanwhile, melt the remaining butter in a skillet and sauté mushrooms.

7. Add flour, salt and pepper. Blend in.

8. Add milk to the mushrooms slowly, stirring until it boils.

9. Add wine and cook for 5 minutes over a low flame.

10. Put the chicken on a plate and pour the sauce over it.

Chapter 03: Seafood and Fish Recipes

Seared Salmon & Green Potato Salad

Cooking time: 40 minutes

Serving size: 2 servings

Description: This gourmet meal is full of delicious flavors. The pickled mustard seeds make it even more delicious.

Ingredients:

- 2 Salmon Fillets (Skin-On)
- Salt
- Pepper
- Olive oil
- Sliced fingerling Potatoes (½ Pound)
- 1 Stalk Celery (sliced)
- Spinach (3 ounces)
- 1 Scallion (sliced)
- Sugar (2 tbsp.)
- Apple Cider Vinegar (2 tbsp.)
- Mustard Seeds (1 tbsp.)
- Prepared Horseradish (1 ½ tsp)
- Sour Cream (¼ Cup)

Directions:

1. Cook mustard seeds in a dry non-stick pan over medium-high heat. Stir the seeds until roasted.

2. Add vinegar, 2 ½ cups of water and sugar. Sprinkle salt and pepper. Boil.

3. Keep boiling for 20 minutes until the seeds are double their size and the liquid has become thick.

4. Transfer to a bowl. Let the seeds pickle.

5. Boil water and salt. Boil sliced potatoes in it for 10 minutes. Drain when tender.

6. Heat 2 tsp of olive oil. Cook spinach until wilted. Season with salt and pepper.

7. Strain the spinach. Release most of the liquid pressing down with a spoon.

8. Chop the spinach.

9. Sprinkle salt and pepper on salmon fillets.

10. Heat 2 tsp of olive oil and cook each side of the salmon fillets for 3 minutes.

11. Add celery, scallions, spinach, horseradish and sour cream in the potatoes. Mix.

12. Serve with salmon fillets topped with mustard seeds.

German Fish with Sauerkraut

Cooking time: 1 hour and 5 minutes

Serving size: 6 servings

Description: If you love seafood, you would not be able to say no to this one!

Ingredients:

- Frozen flounder fillets (1 Pound)
- Cooked sliced mushrooms (1 Cup)
- Drained sauerkraut (1 pound)
- Minced cooked carrots (1/2 cup)
- Condensed cream of potato soup (10 ½ ounces)
- Milk (7 1/2 ounces)
- Minced onion (1/4 tsp)
- Dill seed (1/8 tsp)
- Chopped cooked ham (1 cup)
- Salt
- Pepper
- Grated parmesan cheese (3 tbsp.)
- Minced fresh parsley (1 tbsp.)

Directions:

1. Set your oven at 350°F.

2. Make 2-inches wide strips from fish fillets.

3. Combine mushrooms and sauerkraut in a bowl.

4. Spread this mixture in a baking dish evenly.

5. Sprinkle carrots on it.

6. Set the fish on the top.

7. Mix milk, dill seed, ham, onion, potato soup, salt and pepper in a saucepan.

8. Boil for 1 minute. Pour on the fish in the baking pan.

9. Garnish with a lot of Parmesan and parsley.

10. Cover the pan and bake for 35 minutes.

11. Serve hot when done.

German Beer Fish (Bier Fisch)

Cooking time: 35 minutes

Serving size: 4 servings

Description: Rich in sodium and proteins, you would fall in love with this dish.

Ingredients:

- Butter/Margarine (2 tbsp.)
- Pounded whole carp boneless fillets (3 pounds)
- 1 stalk celery (chopped)
- 1 medium onion (chopped)
- Salt (1/2 tsp)
- 6 peppercorns
- 3 whole cloves
- 1 bay leaf
- 4 lemon slices
- Beer (12 ounces)
- 6 crushed gingersnaps
- Sugar (1 tbsp.)
- Fresh parsley (1 tbsp.)
- Boiled potatoes

Directions:

1. Cut off the head from the fish. On a flat surface, break the bones of the fish.

2. Melt butter in a skillet. Add celery, onion, cloves, peppercorns and salt. Stir.

3. Put bay leaf and lemon slices on top.

4. Place the fish on it.

5. Pour bear over the fish and let it simmer for 20 minutes.

6. Remove from heat. Transfer the fish to a platter. Cover to keep warm.

7. Strain the liquid from the vegetables.

8. Cook gingersnaps and sugar in a skillet.

9. Add 1 ½ cups of the liquid strained from the veggies. Stir until thick.

10. Garnish with parsley and serve the fish with sauce and boiled potatoes.

Bavarian Smelts

Cooking time: 1 hour and 10 minutes

Serving size: 6 servings

Description: This dish is extra delicious and it's really, really simple.

Ingredients:

- Smelts (2 Pounds)
- Flour (1 cup)
- Salt (1 tsp)
- Pepper (1/4 tsp)
- Beer (12 Ounces)
- Fat (1 1/2 cups)
- 3 lemon wedges

Directions:

1. Remove heads from the smelts. Clean them.

2. In a large bowl, pour beer over the smelts. Cover with plastic wrap. Refrigerate for an hour.

3. Heat fat in a skillet.

4. Mix salt and pepper in the flour.

5. Coat the smelts with the mixture.

6. Dip in the beer and coat with the flour once more.

7. Fry the smelts in the melted fat. Fry each side for 5 minutes.

8. Serve with lemon wedges.

Eel in Dill Sauce

Cooking time: 55 minutes

Serving size: 4 servings

Description: This recipe is rich in vitamins, proteins, calcium, sodium and fibers. It's healthy as well as tasty.

Ingredients:

- Boned Eel (7 1/2 Pounds)
- Stock (1/2 Cup)
- White wine (1/2 cup)
- 1 onion
- 1 lemon
- 1 pinch of sugar
- Dill (1 tbsp.)
- Salt
- Freshly ground pepper
- Sour cream (1 cup)

Directions:

1. Have your oven heat up at 425F.

2. Marinate the fish with lemon juice and salt. Set aside.

3. Place the fish in a soaked romertopf.

4. Add wine and stock to it. Sprinkle salt, sugar and pepper.

5. Add chopped onion, cover it and cook it for 40 minutes.

6. Mix sour cream and dill. Add the mixture to the romertopf.

7. Bake for 5 minutes.

8. Serve with salad potatoes if you like.

Chapter 04: Sauces and Salads

Jägerschnitzel Sauce

Cooking time: 15 minutes

Serving size: 4 servings

Description: This is a divine German sauce that you can enjoy with the Schnitzels.

Ingredients:

- Butter (1 tbsp.)
- Sliced mushrooms (1 lb.)
- 1 diced onion
- 3 slices diced bacon
- Tomato paste (2 tbsp.)
- White wine (1 cup)
- Water (1 cup)
- Salt
- Pepper
- Thyme
- Paprika (2 tbsp.)
- Chopped parsley (2 tbsp.)
- Sour cream (1/4 cup)

Directions:

1. Brown onion and bacon in 1 tbsp. of butter in a skillet.

2. Add mushrooms and fry.

3. Add tomato paste, wine and water.

4. Add paprika, salt, pepper and thyme.

5. Boil and then simmer for 5 minutes until the sauce thickens.

6. Add parsley. Serve!

German Zigeunerschnitzel

Cooking time: 40 minutes

Serving size: 4 servings

Description: This is a hot paprika sauce that you can serve with pork chops, schnitzel etc.

Ingredients:

- Oil (1 tbsp.)
- 2 pressed garlic cloves
- Flour (1 ½ tbsp.)
- 1 can chicken broth (1 14 oz.)
- 1 sliced medium onion
- 3 sliced peppers (red, yellow or orange)
- Ground Sweet Hungarian paprika (2 tsp)
- Ground Hot Hungarian paprika (1 - 2 tsp)
- Tomato paste (2 tbsp.)
- Salt and pepper to taste
- Sugar or honey (2 tsp)

Directions:

1. Sauté onion slices in a pan.

2. Add peppers and cook.

3. Add garlic and sprinkle flour and paprika and cook for 2 minutes.

4. Little by little, add the broth. Keep stirring until thick.

5. Cool the mixture for 20 minutes.

6. Add lemon juice, salt, pepper and sugar according to your taste.

German Green Sauce (Grune Sosse)

Cooking time: 2 minutes

Serving size: 4 servings

Description: This German sauce is very delicious with boiled vegetables. The unique herbs and the sour cream give it a distinct taste that you will just love.

Ingredients:

- Plain Greek yogurt (1/2 cup)
- Buttermilk (1/2 cup)
- Walnut oil (1 1/2 tsp)
- 1 hard-boiled egg yolk
- Sour cream (1/2 cup)
- Fresh lemon juice (2 tbsp.)
- Packed parsley (2 cups)
- Finely chopped chives (1 cup)
- Packed watercress (1 1/2 cups)
- Packed sorrel (1 cup)
- Kosher salt (to taste)
- Freshly ground black pepper (to taste)

Directions:

1. Process all the above-mentioned ingredients, save for Kosher salt and black pepper, in a blender until the mixture is smooth,

2. Season with salt and pepper.

Sauerkraut Salad

Cooking time: 10 minutes

Serving size: 4 to 6 servings

Description: This salad is the yummiest German salad. The main ingredient, sauerkraut, is very good for your immune system.

Ingredients:

- 1 large can sauerkraut (2 - 3 cups)
- Olive oil (1/4 cup)
- Granulated sugar (1/2 cup)
- 1 large coarsely grated carrot
- 1 diced red pepper
- 1/2 diced onion
- 2 diced stalks celery
- Salt (according to your taste)
- Pepper (according to your taste)

Directions:

1. Use a sieve over a bowl to drain sauerkraut.

2. Reserve half cup of the liquid.

3. Mix sugar with sauerkraut in a large bowl. Let it sit for 15 minutes.

4. Add the reserved sauerkraut liquid and oil.

5. Add the rest of the ingredients.

6. Sprinkle salt and pepper over the salad.

7. Refrigerate for hours before serving.

Warm German Potato Salad

Cooking time: 15 minutes

Serving size: 2 servings

Description: This tangy and warm salad is blissful if you eat with sandwiches and burgers.

Ingredients:

- All-purpose flour (2 tsp)
- 2 diced bacon strips
- Refrigerated sliced potatoes (2 cups)
- Minced fresh parsley (1 tbsp.)
- 1 chopped small onion
- Water (1/2 cup)
- Cider vinegar (2 tbsp.)
- Diced pimientos (2 tbsp.)
- Sugar (4 tsp)
- Salt (1/4 tsp)

Directions:

1. Cook the bacon in a large skillet until it is crisp.

2. Remove the bacon to paper towels.

3. Sauté onion until translucent. Add flour. Stir to blend.

4. Add vinegar, sugar, parsley, salt and water. Boil.

5. Stir until it thickens.

6. Cook potatoes in water in the meantime.

7. Drain when tender.

8. Add the pimientos, potatoes and bacon to the sauce.

9. Toss to mix well.

Chapter 05: Delicious Desserts

German Baby

Cooking time: 25 minutes

Serving size: 2 servings

Description: This is a really quick desserts recipe that you can enjoy with warm maple syrup, jam and lemon wedges.

Ingredients:

- 3 eggs
- Milk (3/4 cup)
- All-purpose flour (3/4 cup)
- Butter (1/4 cup)
- Confectioners' sugar (2 tbsp.)

Directions:

1. Set your oven at 425F.

2. In a 10-inch cast iron skillet, place butter and heat it in the oven.

3. Using an electric beater, whisk eggs at high speed.

4. Slowly add flour and milk. Whisk.

5. Pour the mixture into the skillet. Bake for 20 minutes in the oven.

6. Like a soufflé, it will rise but when you take it out, it will fall.

7. Dust with sugar. Enjoy!

German Apple Cake

Cooking time: 1 hour

Serving size: 24 servings

Description: This German apple cake is moist and dense which is extra-delicious.

Ingredients:

- Vegetable oil (1 cup)
- 2 eggs
- Baking soda (1 tsp)
- All-purpose flour (2 cups)
- Ground cinnamon (2 tsp)
- Salt (1/2 tsp)
- White sugar (2 cups)
- Vanilla extract (1 tsp)
- Peeled, diced and cored apples (4 cups)

Directions:

1. Set your oven at 350F.

2. Apply oil and flour on a 9x13 inches cake pan.

3. Beat oil and eggs in a bowl with an electric beater. Add sugar and vanilla and beat well until creamy.

4. In a bowl, mix baking soda, flour, salt and cinnamon.

5. Add this to the egg mixture and mix well.

6. Put apple slices inside the batter.

7. Spread the mixture in the cake pan.

8. Bake in the oven for 45 minutes.

9. Let the cake cool down.

10. Serve with cream cheese frosting.

Old German Honey Cookies

Cooking time: 25 minutes

Serving size: 24 servings

Description: My grandmother used to make this to us when we were kids. I loved and still love these cookies.

Ingredients:

- White sugar (1 cup)
- Shortening (1 cup)
- Honey (1 cup)
- 2 eggs
- Vanilla extract (1 tsp)
- Baking soda (1 tsp)
- All-purpose flour (4 cups)
- Ground ginger (1 tsp)

Directions:

1. Melt sugar, honey and shortening in a saucepan over low heat. Cool it down.

2. Blend together eggs, baking soda, ginger and vanilla.

3. Add the honey mixture slowly.

4. Gradually add 4 cups of flour in the mixture.

5. Stir until well combined.

6. Drop the mixture onto a cookie sheet.

7. Bake at 350F for about 15 minutes or until the cookies are golden.

German Marble Cake

Cooking time: 1 hour and 30 minutes

Serving size: 18 servings

Description: This super-duper delicious cake comes from my mom. She still makes it for me every time I go visit her.

Ingredients:

- Butter (1 cup)
- Sugar (3/4 cups)
- 5 egg yolks
- All-purpose flour (3 1/2 cups)
- Milk (1 cup)
- Baking powder (2 tsp)
- 5 egg whites
- Sweet cocoa (2 tbsp.)

Directions:

1. Preheat your oven to 350F.

2. Apply flour and oil to a 10-inch tube pan.

3. Mix butter with sugar in a large bowl.

4. Add egg yolks in it and beat really well for about 10 minutes.

5. Add flour to the mixture slowly, keep stirring.

6. Add splashes of milk in between stirring.

7. Add baking powder when the mixture is well combined. Stir.

8. Beat egg whites in a separate pot.

9. Mix the egg whites in the batter.

10. Save ¼ of the batter and pour the remaining into the baking pan.

11. Add cocoa powder to the remaining batter that you have saved.

12. Pour into the pan and fold with a fork to get a marbled look.

13. Bake for 70 minutes. Cool down for 10 minutes. Serve!

German Iced Coffee

Cooking time: 5 minutes

Serving size: 4 servings

Description: This one is a really quick recipe especially for coffee lovers.

Ingredients:

- Cold strong coffee (2 cups)
- Vanilla ice cream (8 small scoops)
- Whipped cream

Directions:

1. Take 4 tall glasses and put 2 scoops of ice cream in each glass.

2. Pour coffee on the ice cream.

3. Garnish each glass with a lot of whipped cream.

4. Serve instantly.

Conclusion

Eating the same kind of food everyday can be really boring. I have always found German food really fascinating that's why I want you to try these delicious foods. I hope you will not find it difficult to understand anything in this book. Good luck!

Author's Afterthoughts

Thank you for reading my book. Your feedback is important to us. It would be greatly appreciated if you could please take a moment to *REVIEW* this book on Amazon so that we could make our next version better

Thanks!

Martha Stone

martha@168publishing.com

Made in the USA
Middletown, DE
10 May 2017